A Girl In A Museum World

Tellie Simpson

Illustrations by Morgan Jennings

Cover design and illustrations by Morgan Jennings

Hardback ISBN 979-8-9856268-1-0
Paperback ISBN 979-8-9856268-0-3

Library of Congress Control Number:
2022900897

First Edition April 2022

Published by AGIAMW, LLC
www.Agirlinamuseumworld.com
Baltimore, Maryland

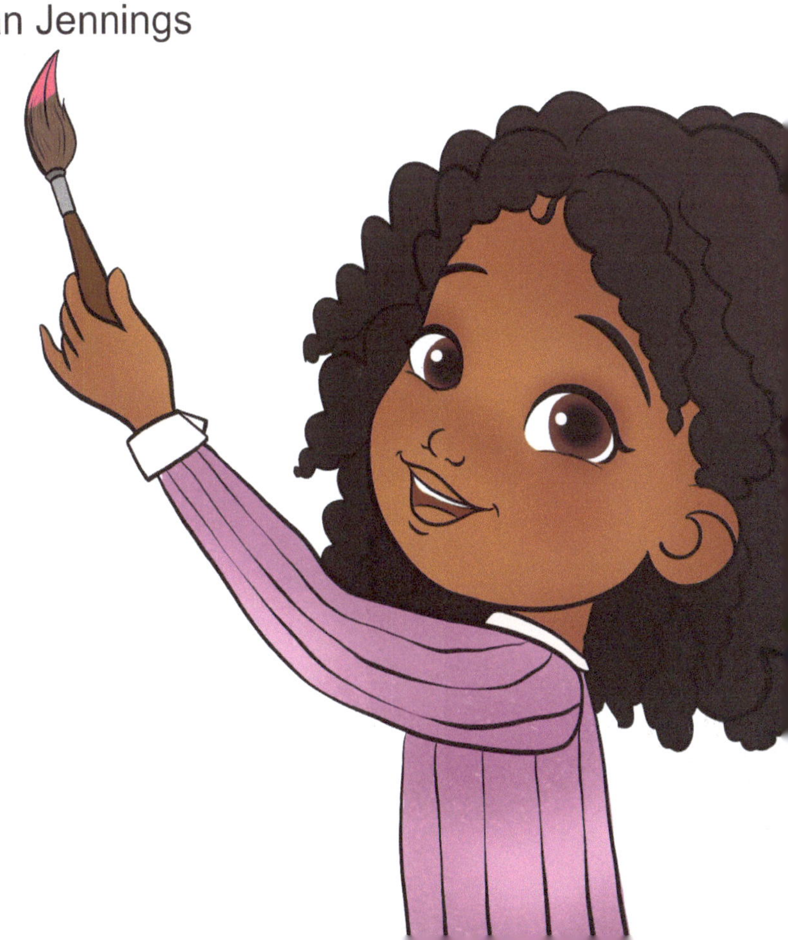

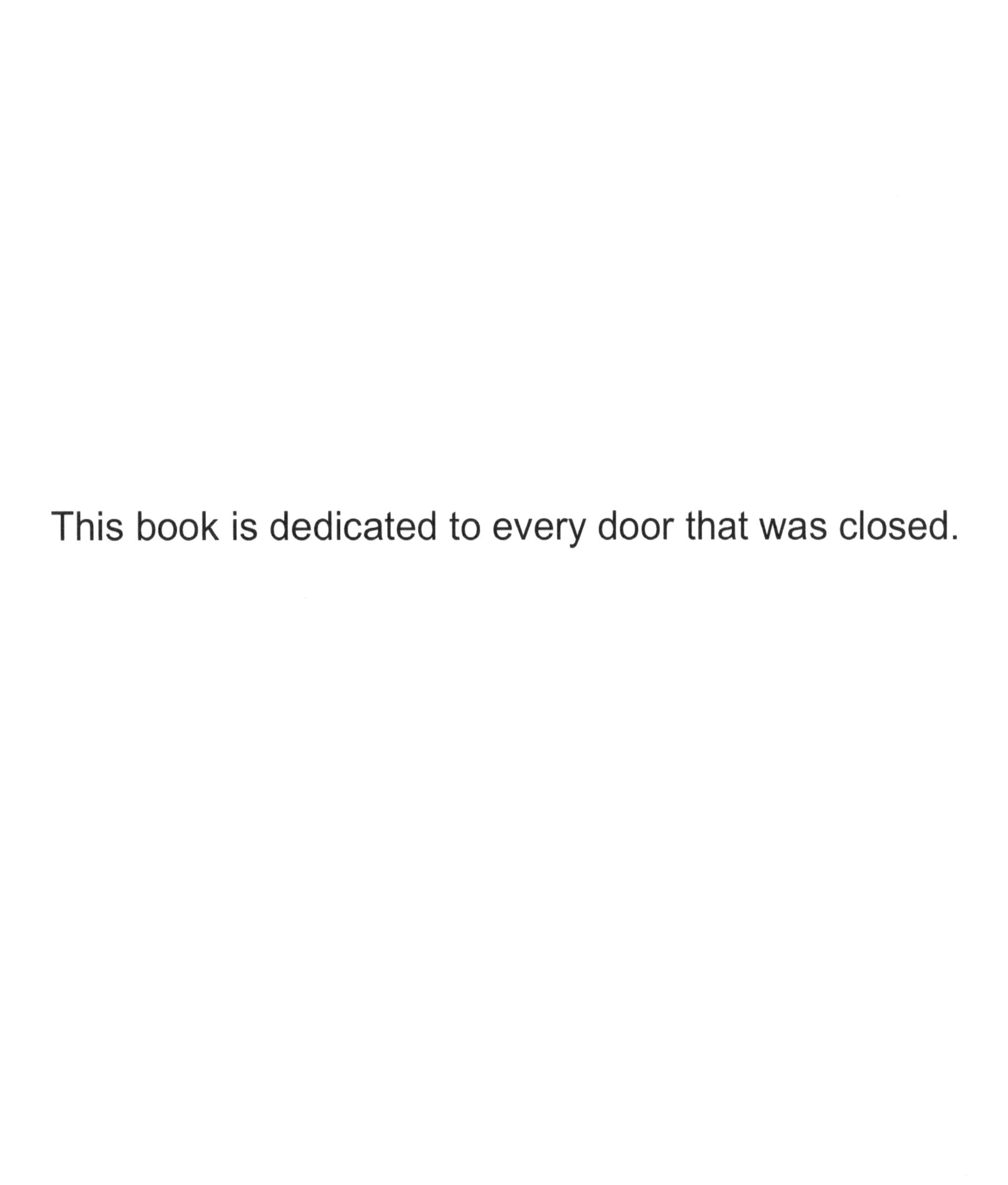

This book is dedicated to every door that was closed.

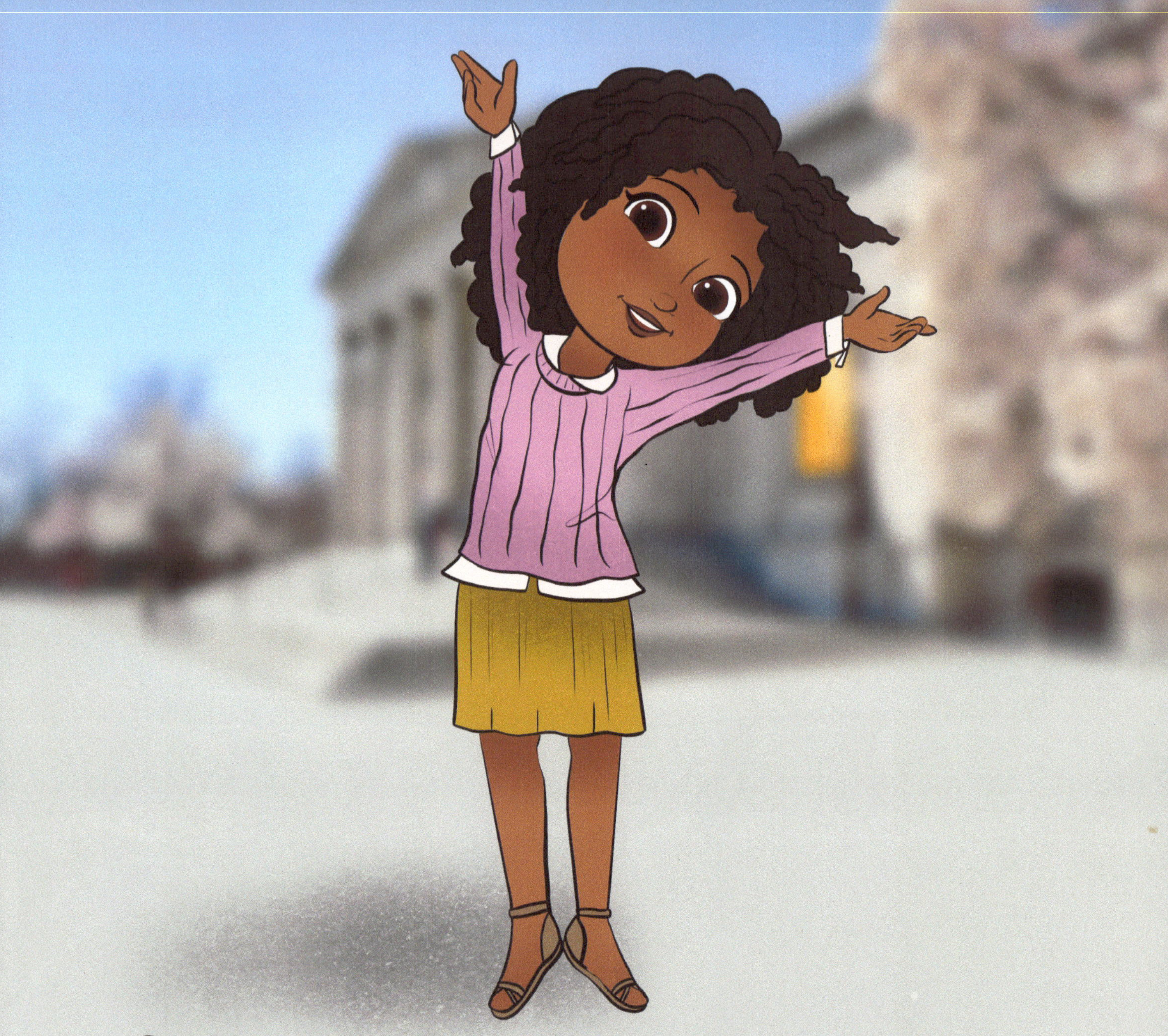

Sophia was so happy. She was jumping with glee.
"I'm going to the Museum to learn about people that look just like me!"

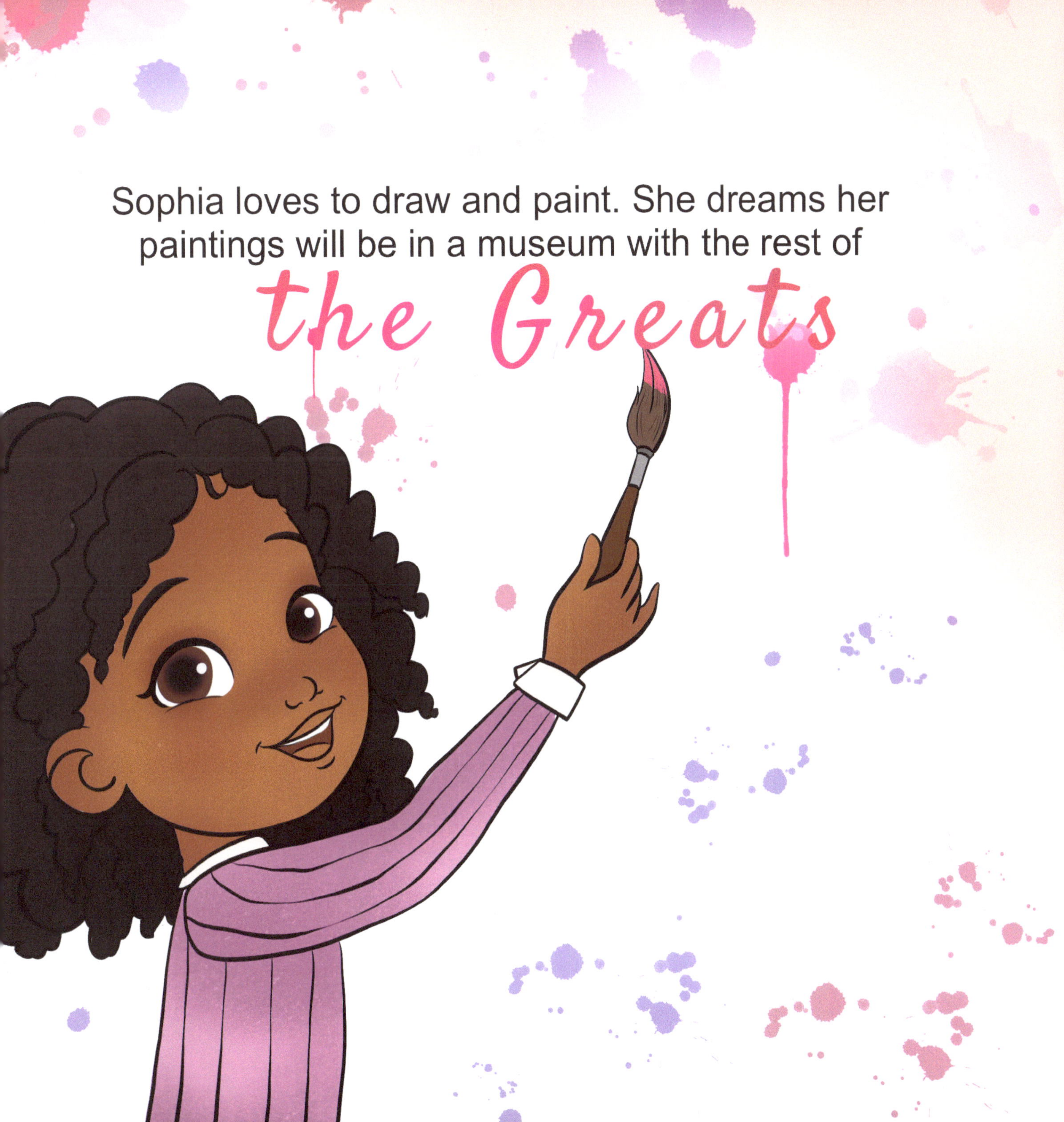

Sophia loves to draw and paint. She dreams her paintings will be in a museum with the rest of

the Greats

Museums have new and old paintings from long,long ago.

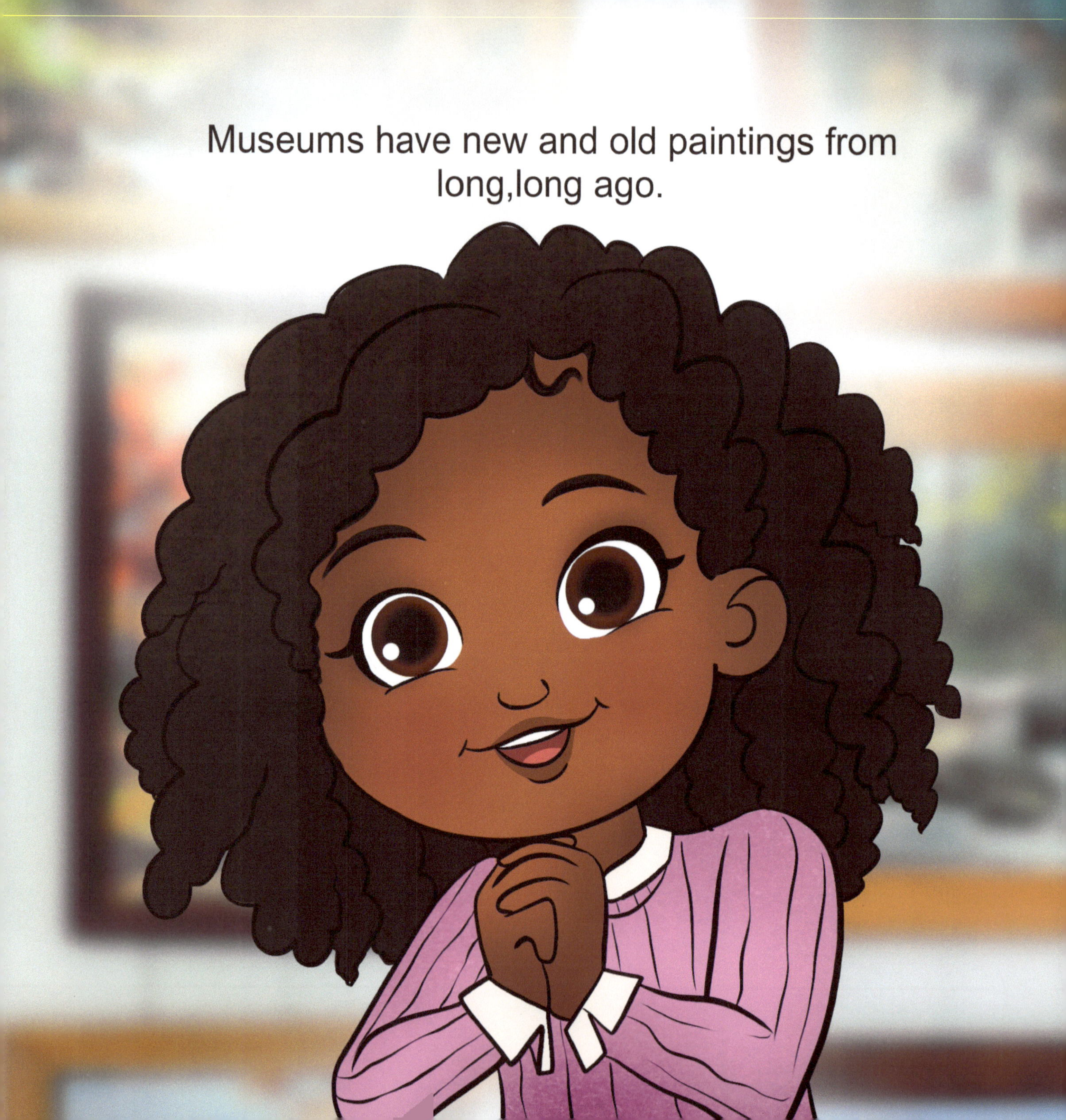

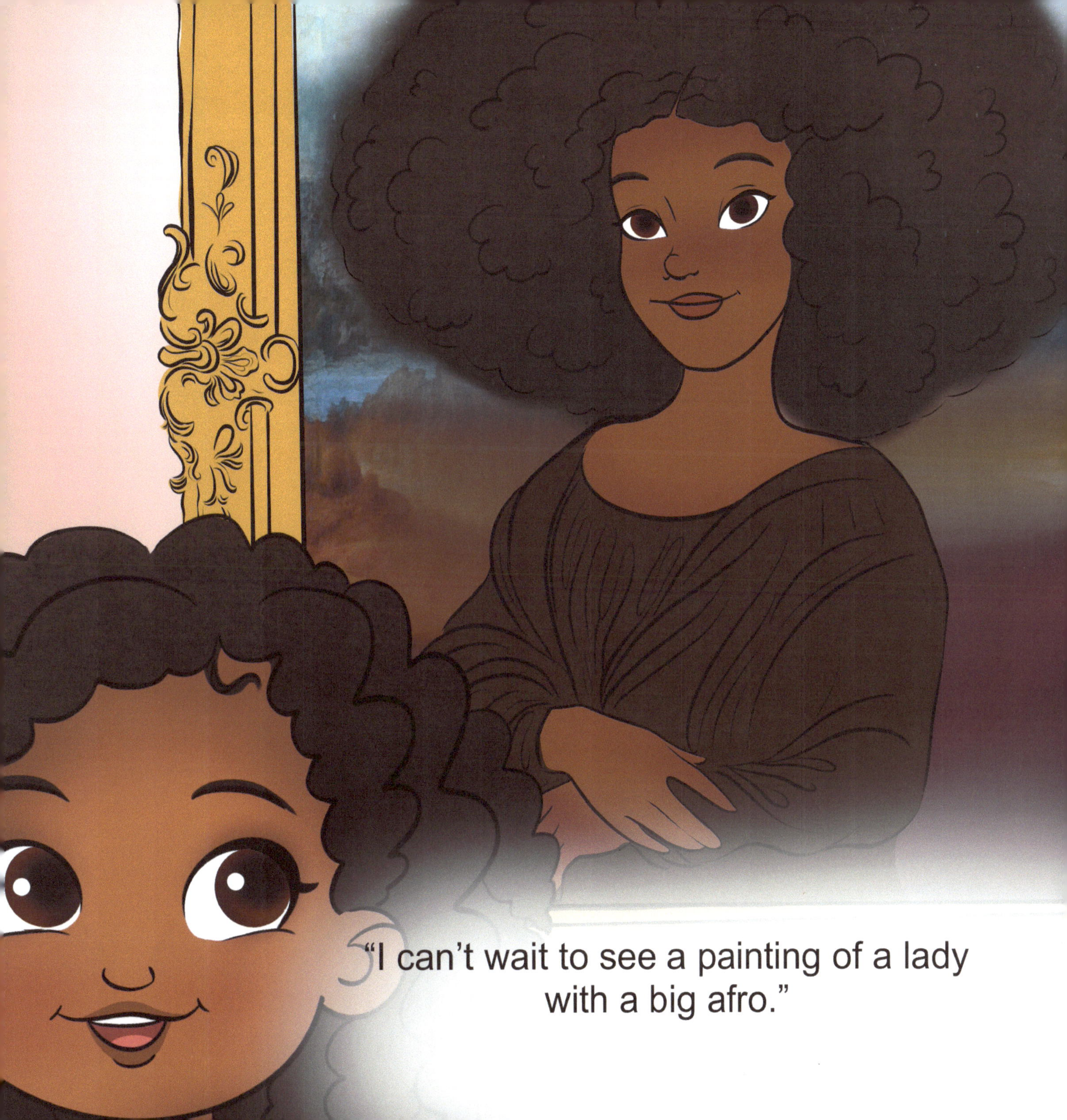

"I can't wait to see a painting of a lady with a big afro."

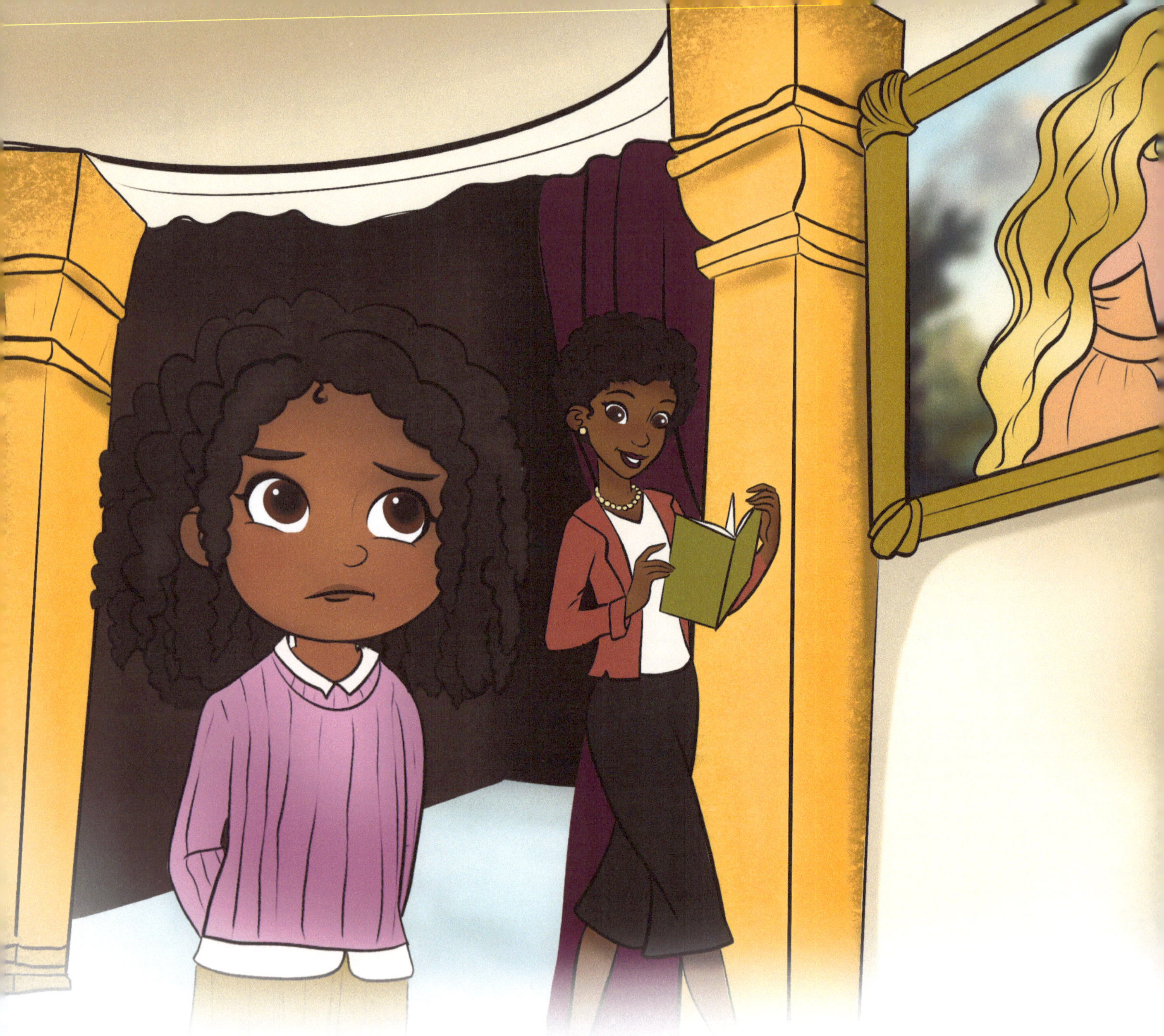

“I can not touch these things, but I can stare. I wonder where is the lady with the big hair?”

Sophia glares at the paintings with her big brown eyes.
But she begins to feel sad inside.

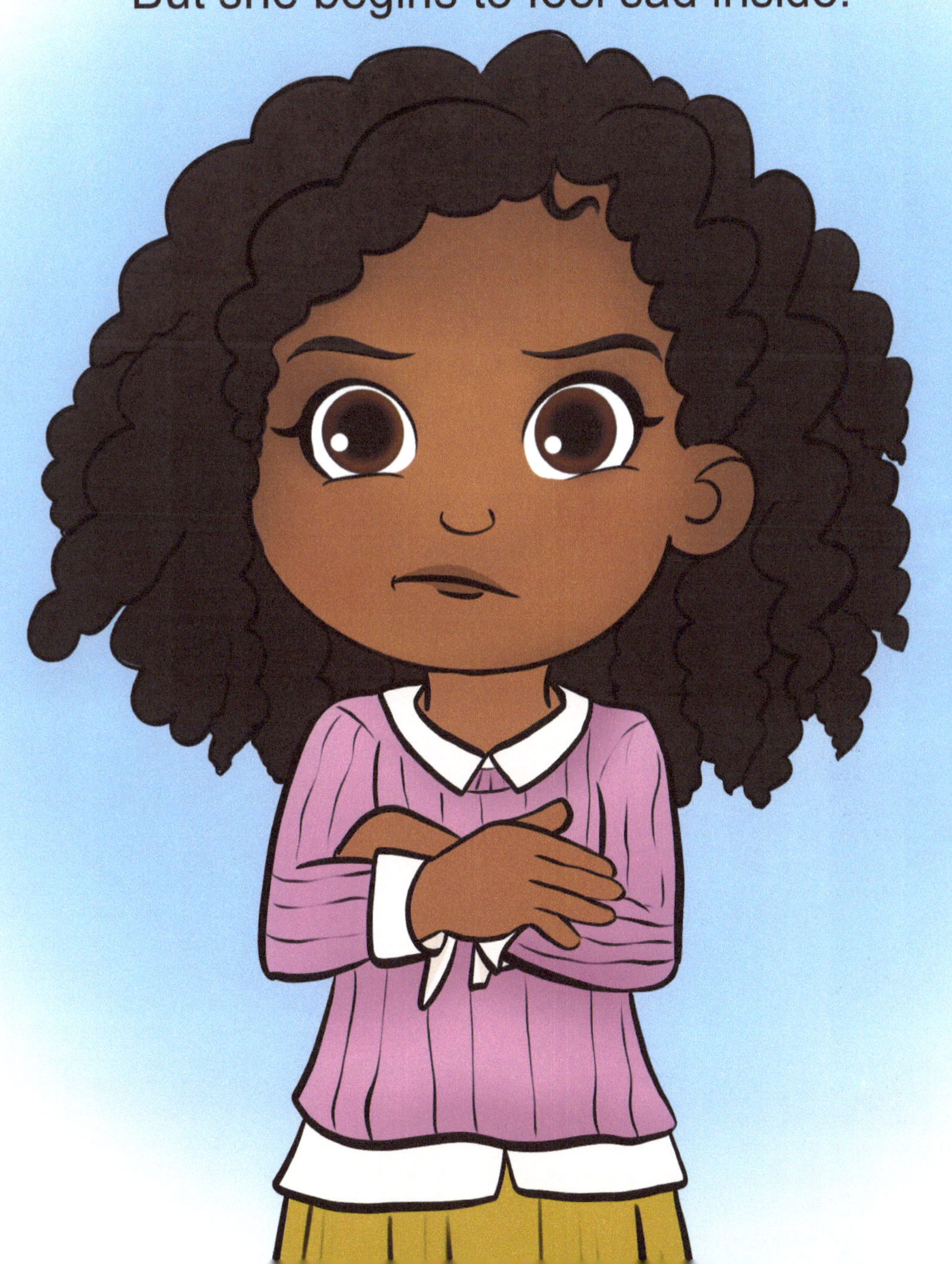

Sophia turns to her mother to ask, “Why are the same people on every wall?

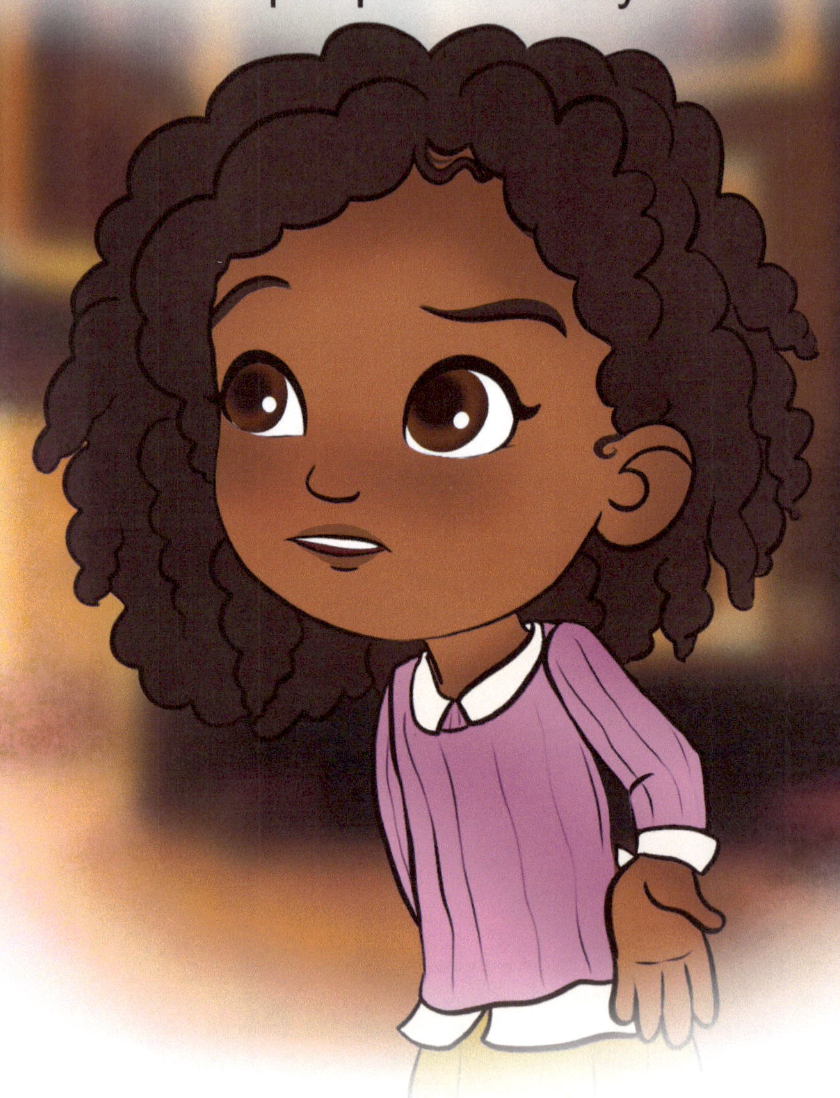

I thought museums were filled with stories for us all.”

Mom holds Sophia’s hand so gentle and sweet.
She says, “Come on, let’s go. You’re in for a treat!”

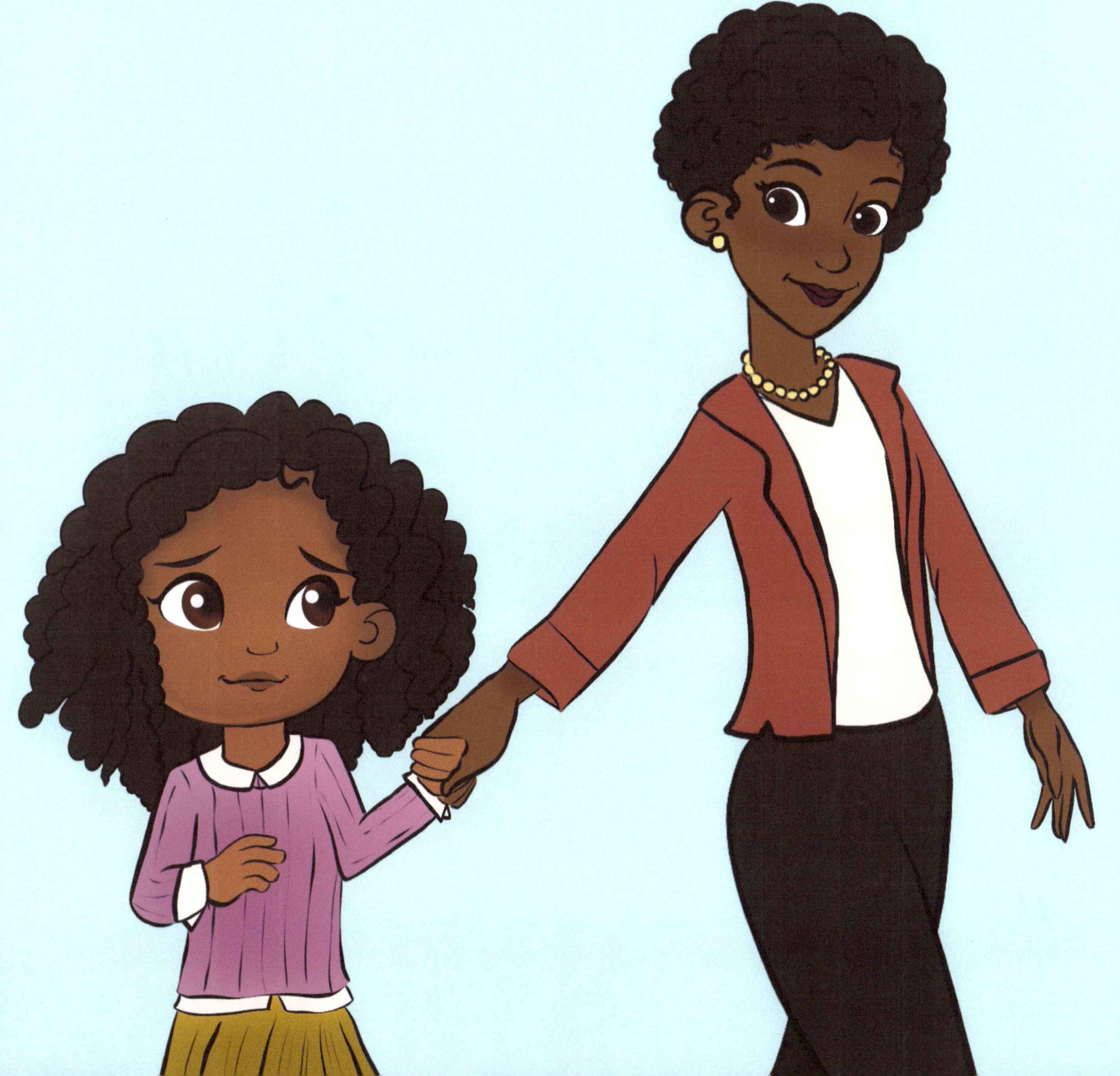

Mom and Sophia drive to the biggest building in the city.

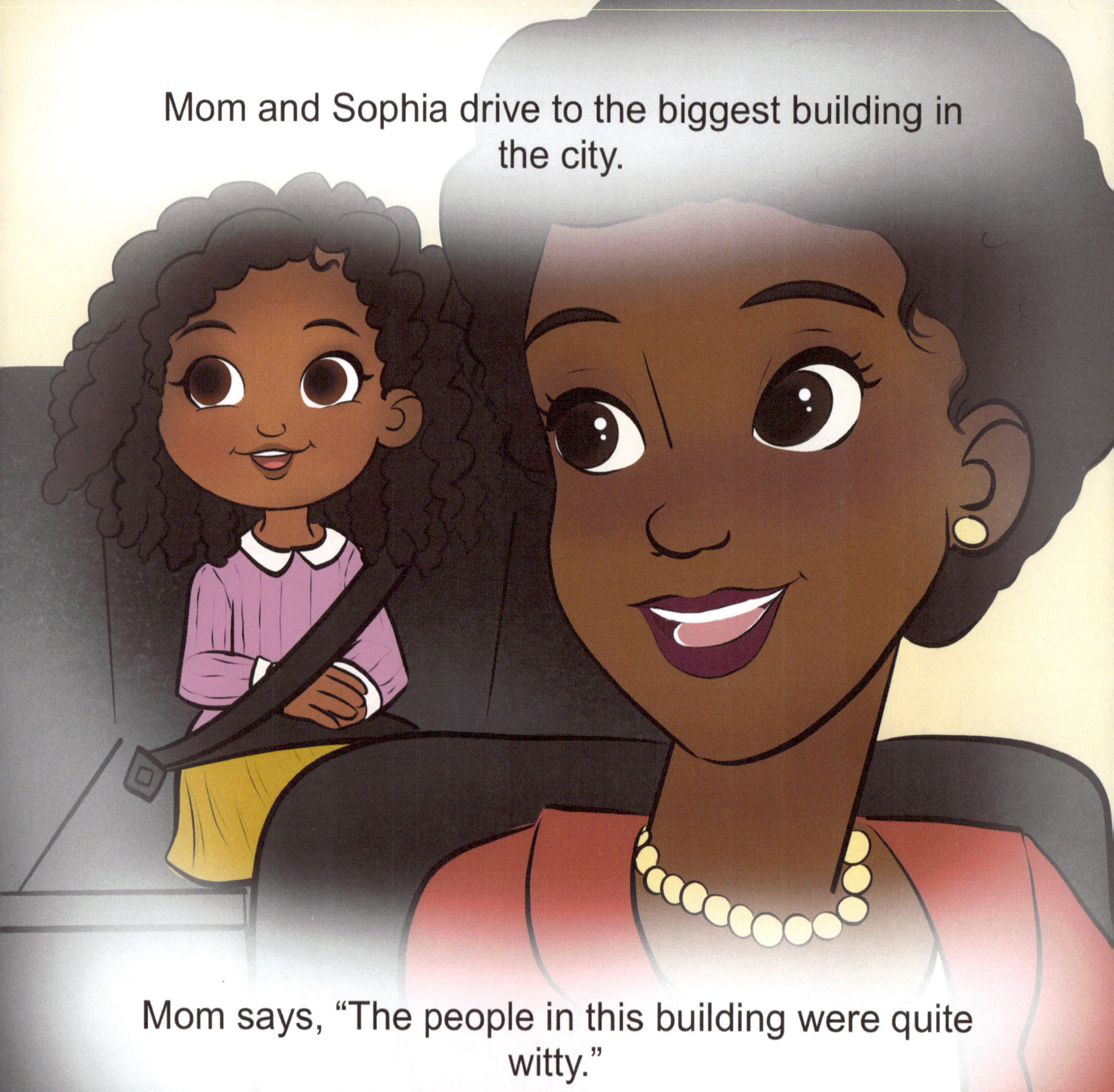

Mom says, “The people in this building were quite witty.”

Sophia sees girls with curly hair, big lips, and pretty brown skin. “They are all so beautiful. I fit right in.”

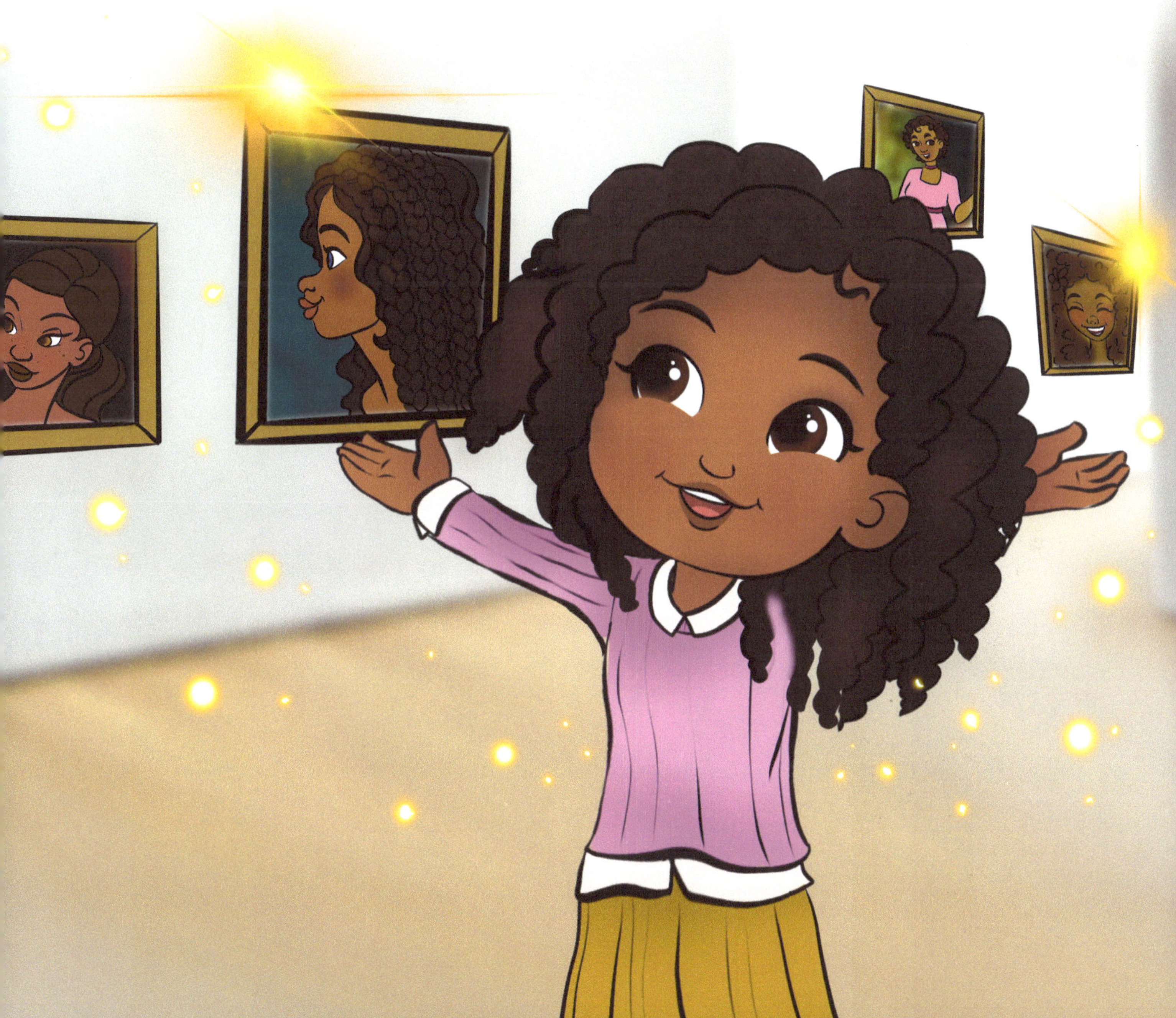

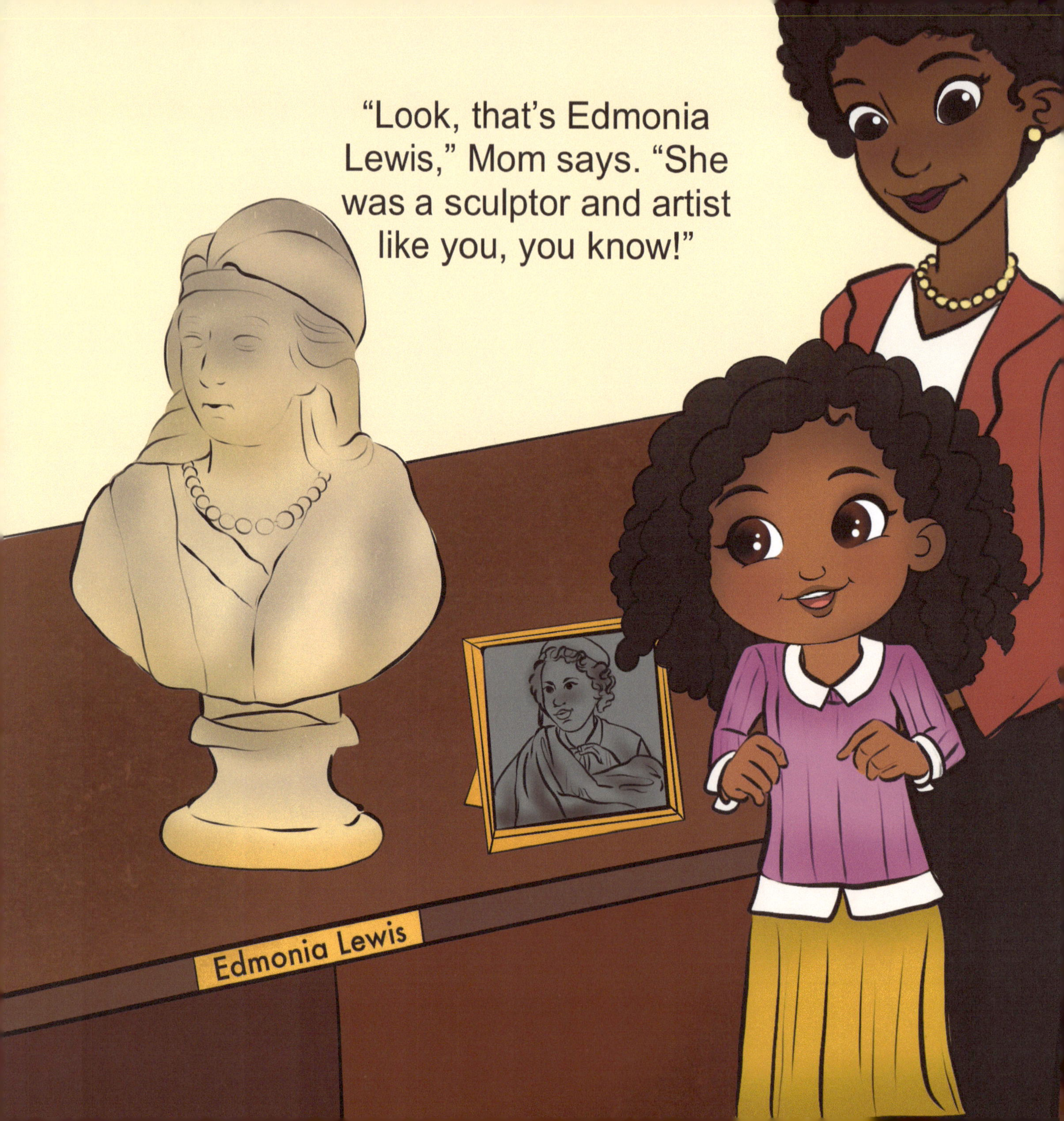

"Look, that's Edmonia Lewis," Mom says. "She was a sculptor and artist like you, you know!"

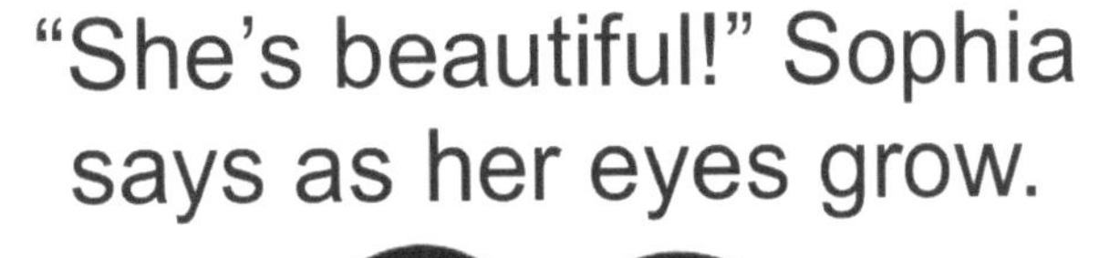

"She's beautiful!" Sophia
says as her eyes grow.

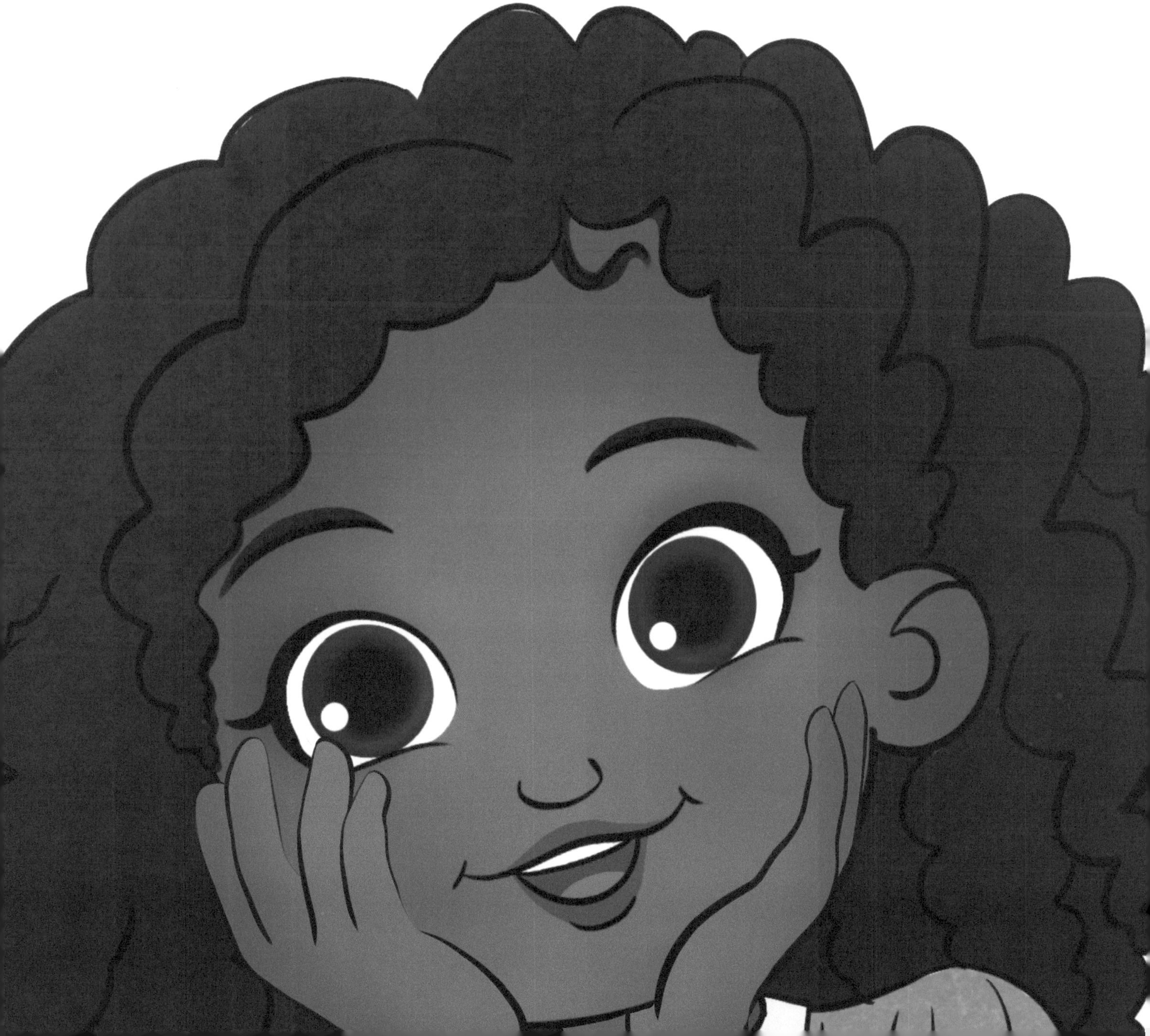

Mom and Sophia make their way home, and Sophia rushes to her desk.

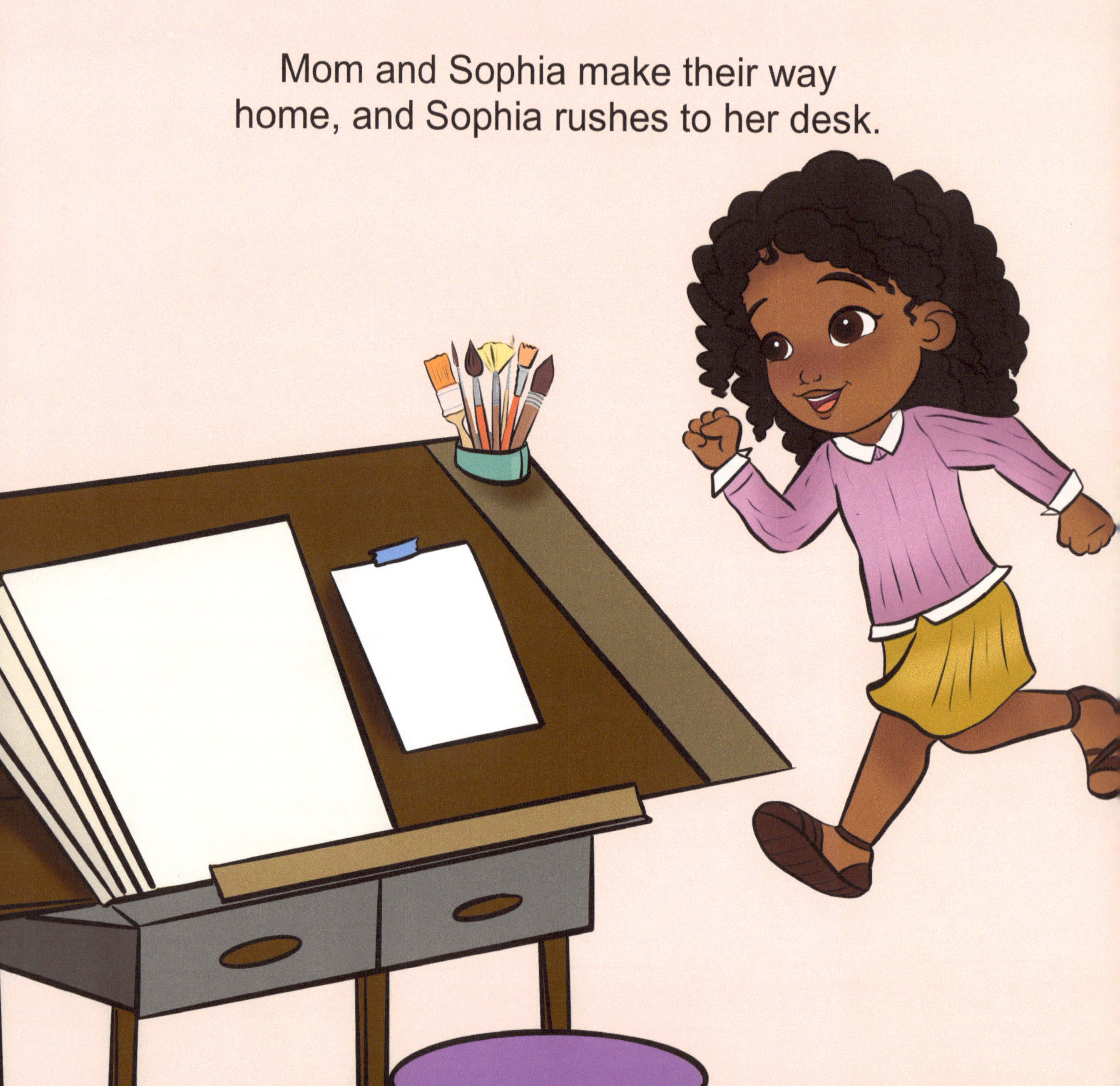

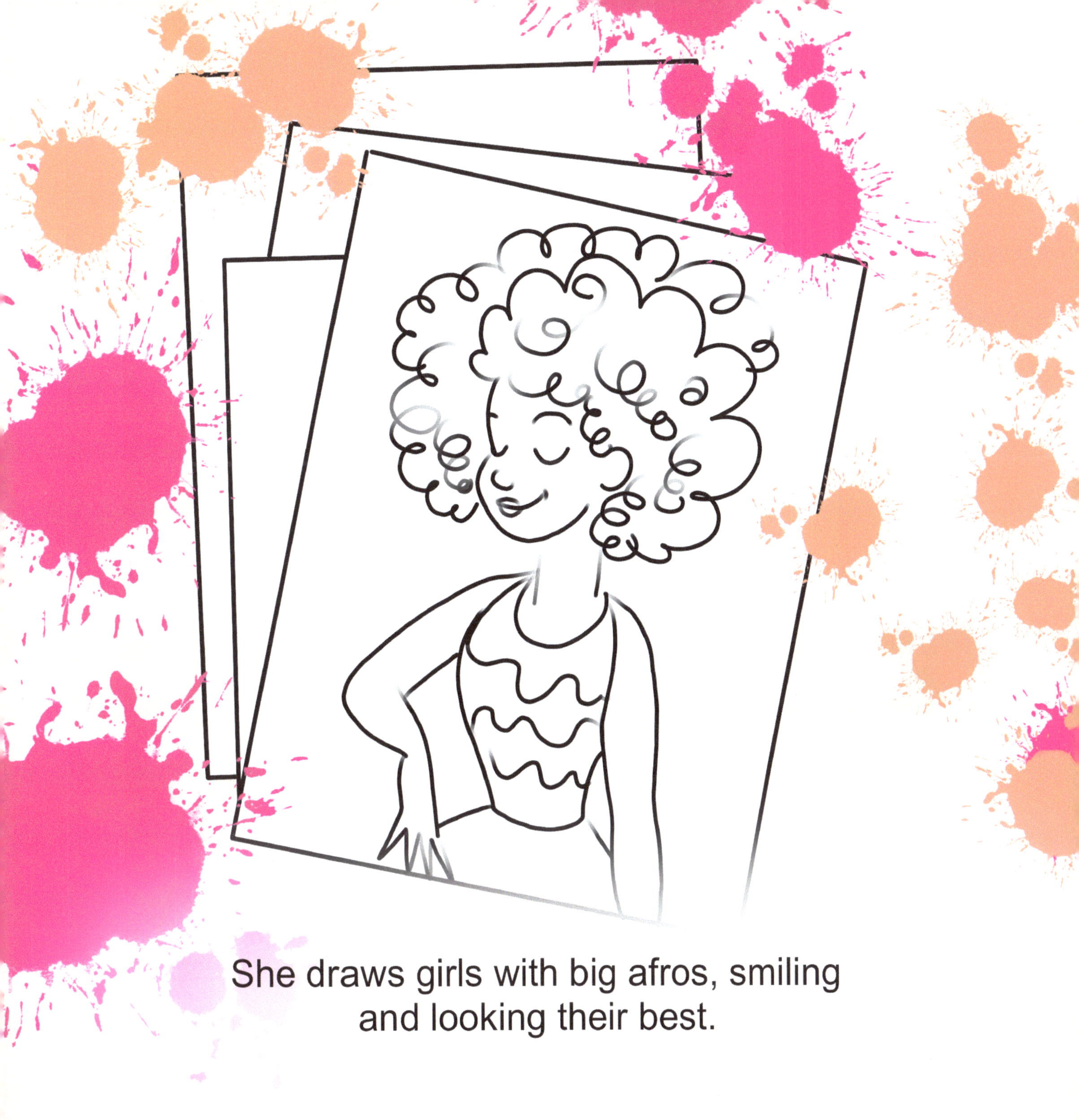

She draws girls with big afros, smiling
and looking their best.

"My drawings and stories will be in every museum!"

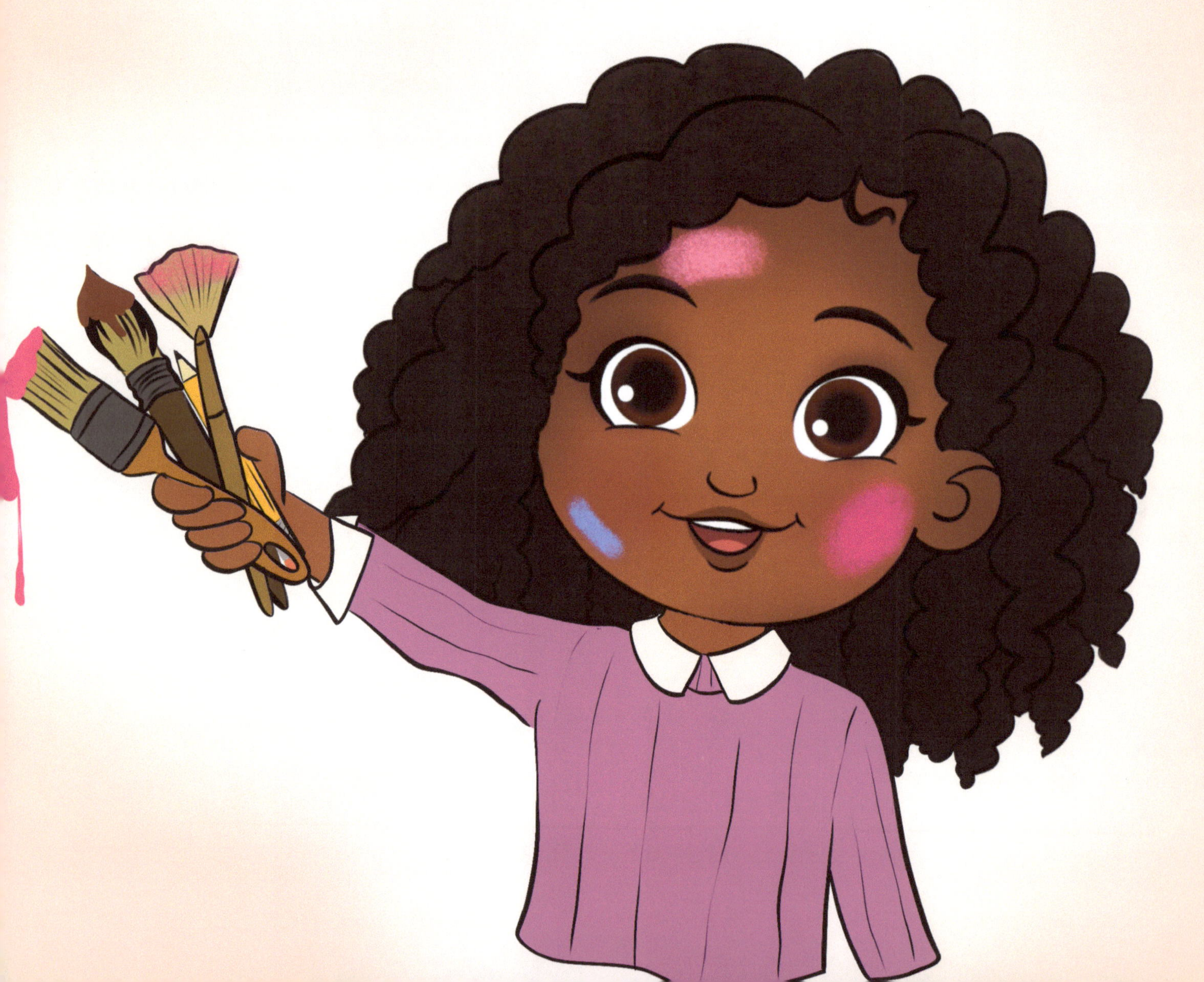

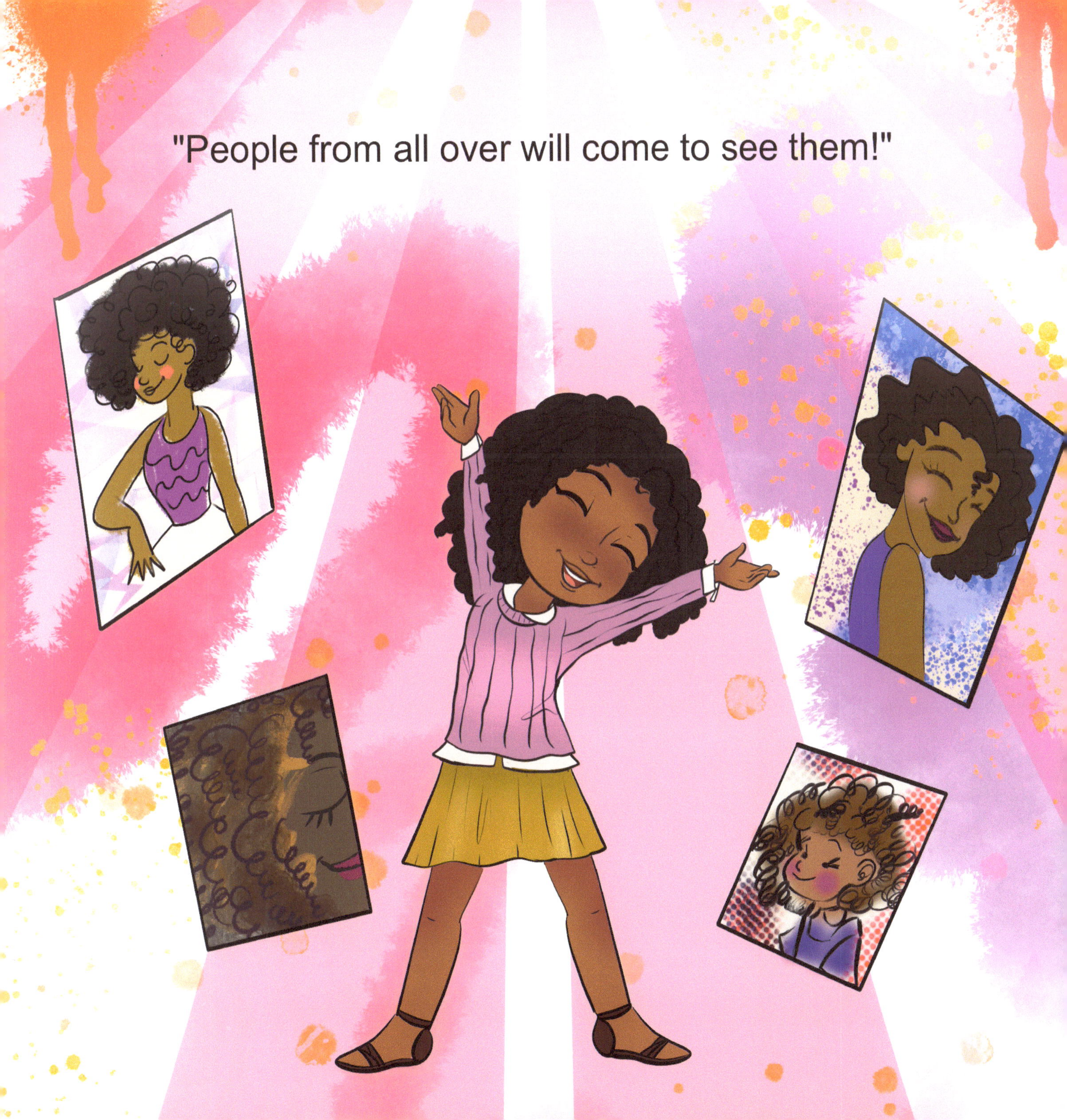

"People from all over will come to see them!"

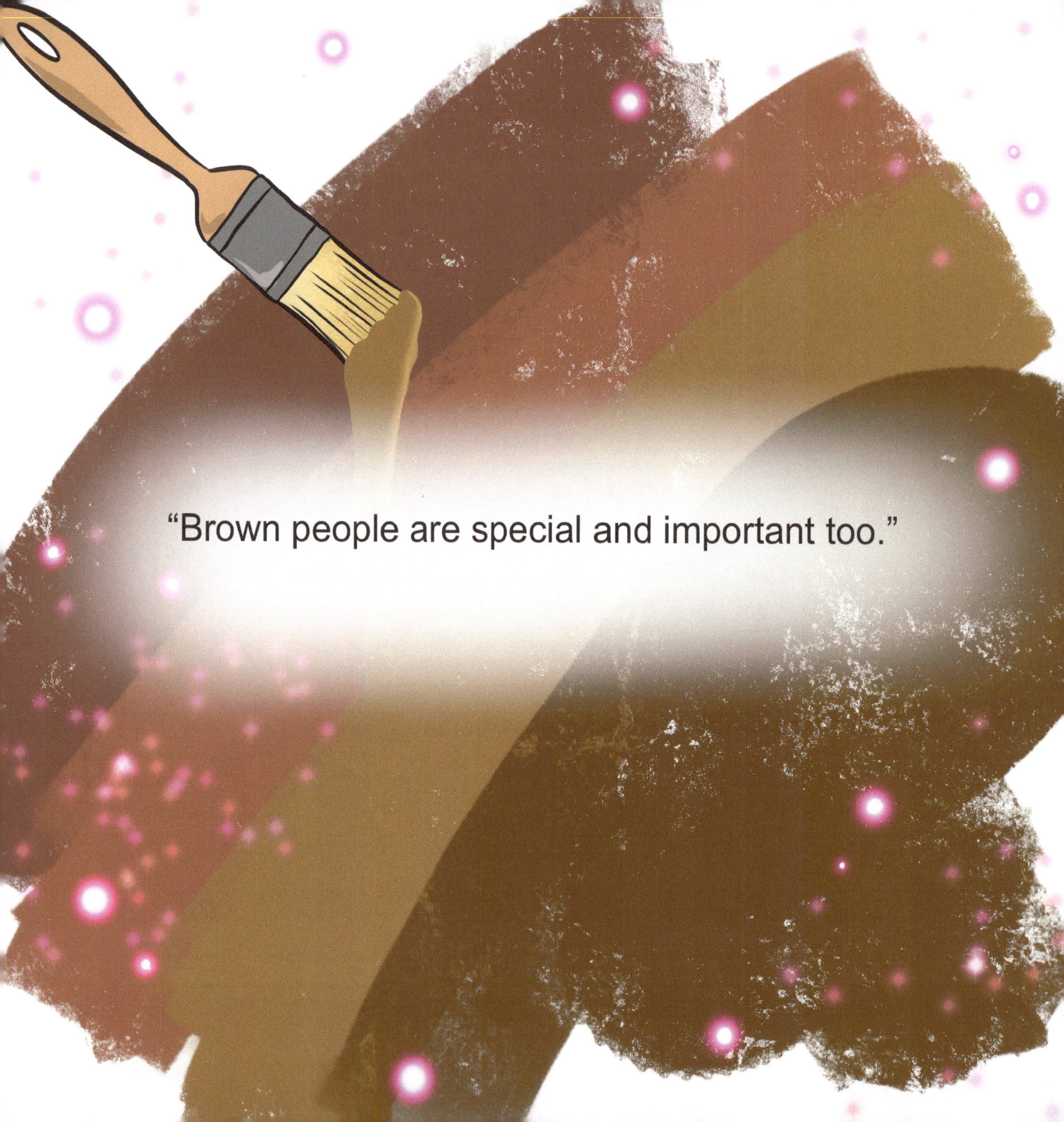

“Brown people are special and important too.”

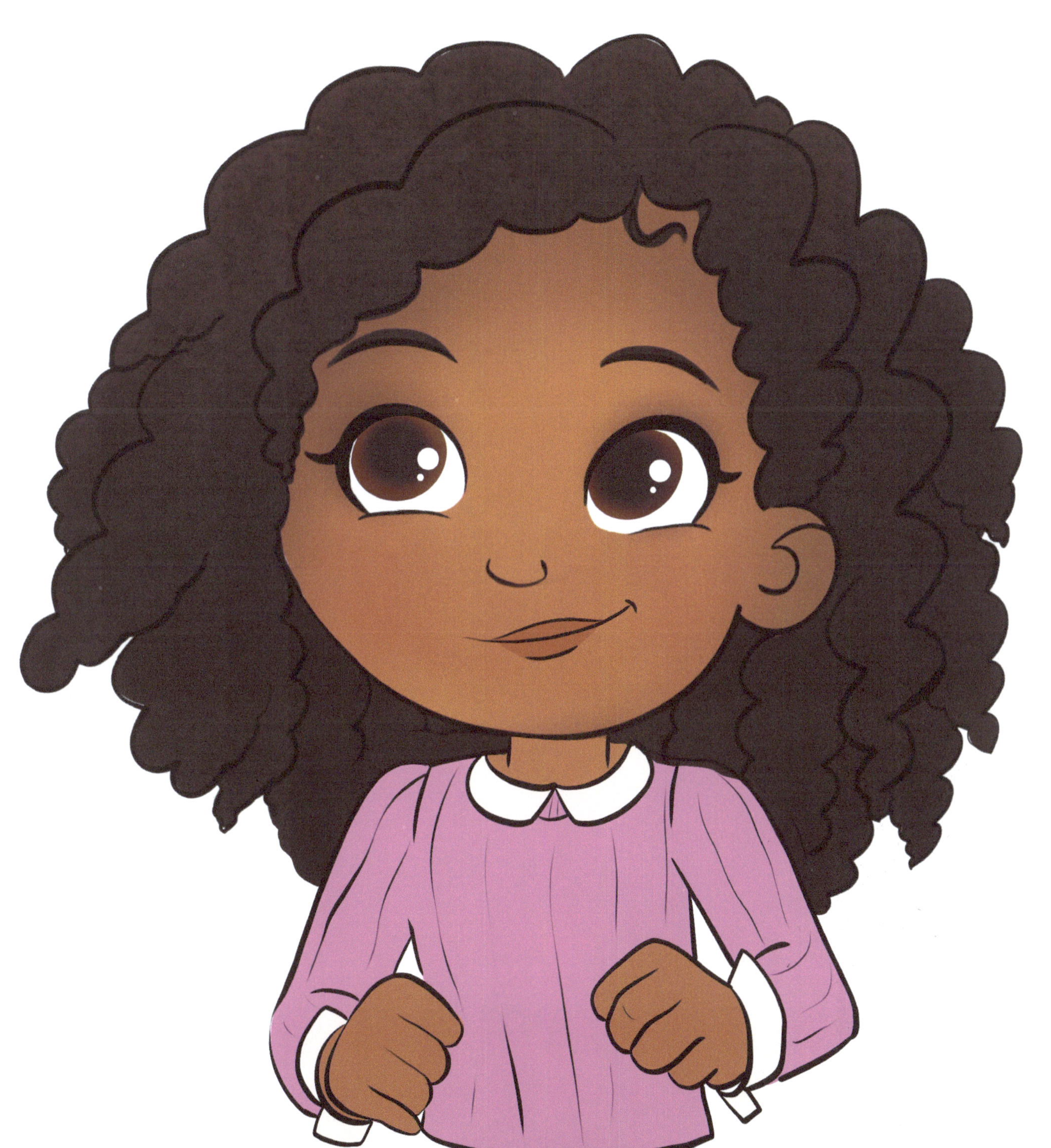

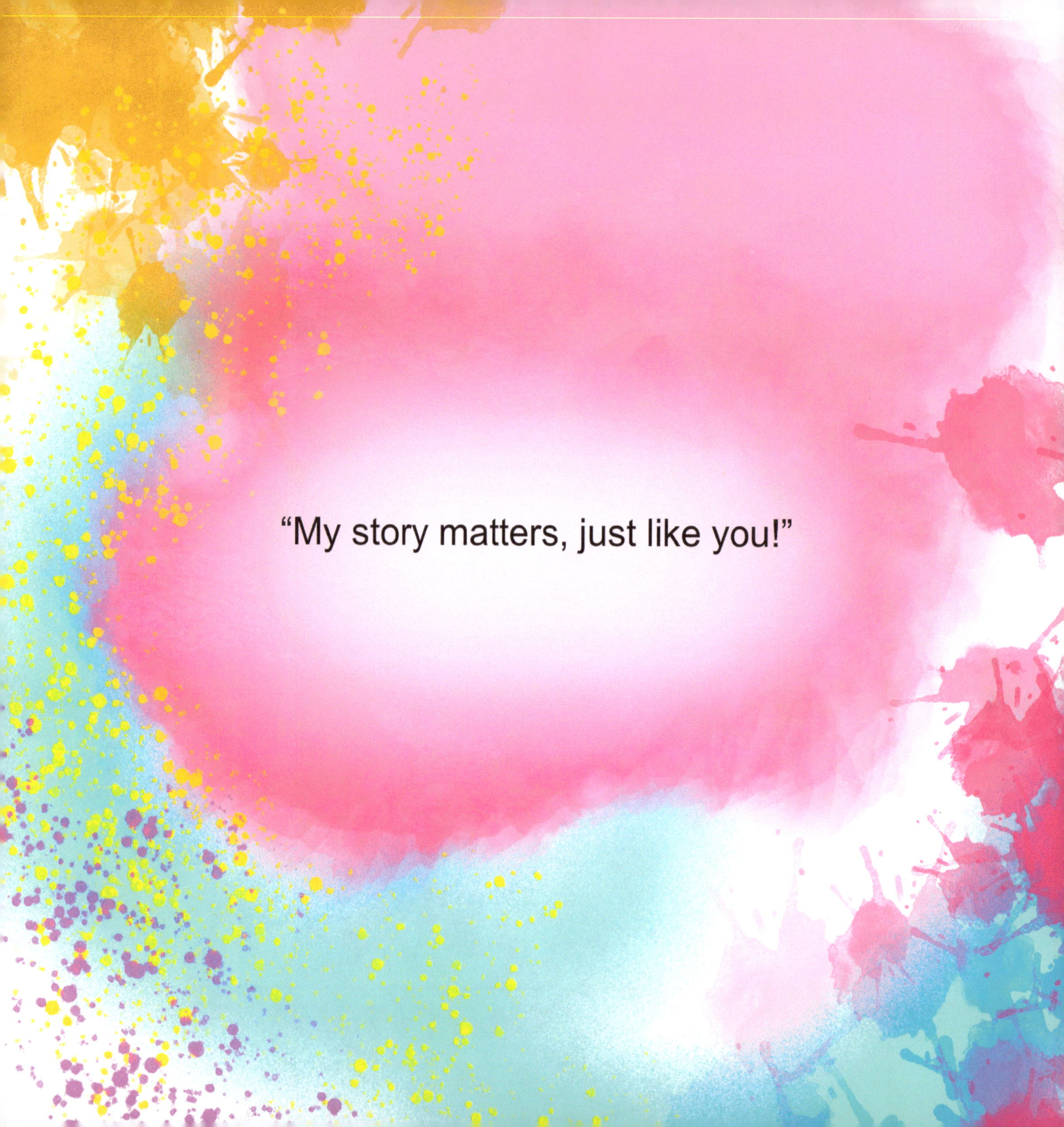

"My story matters, just like you!"

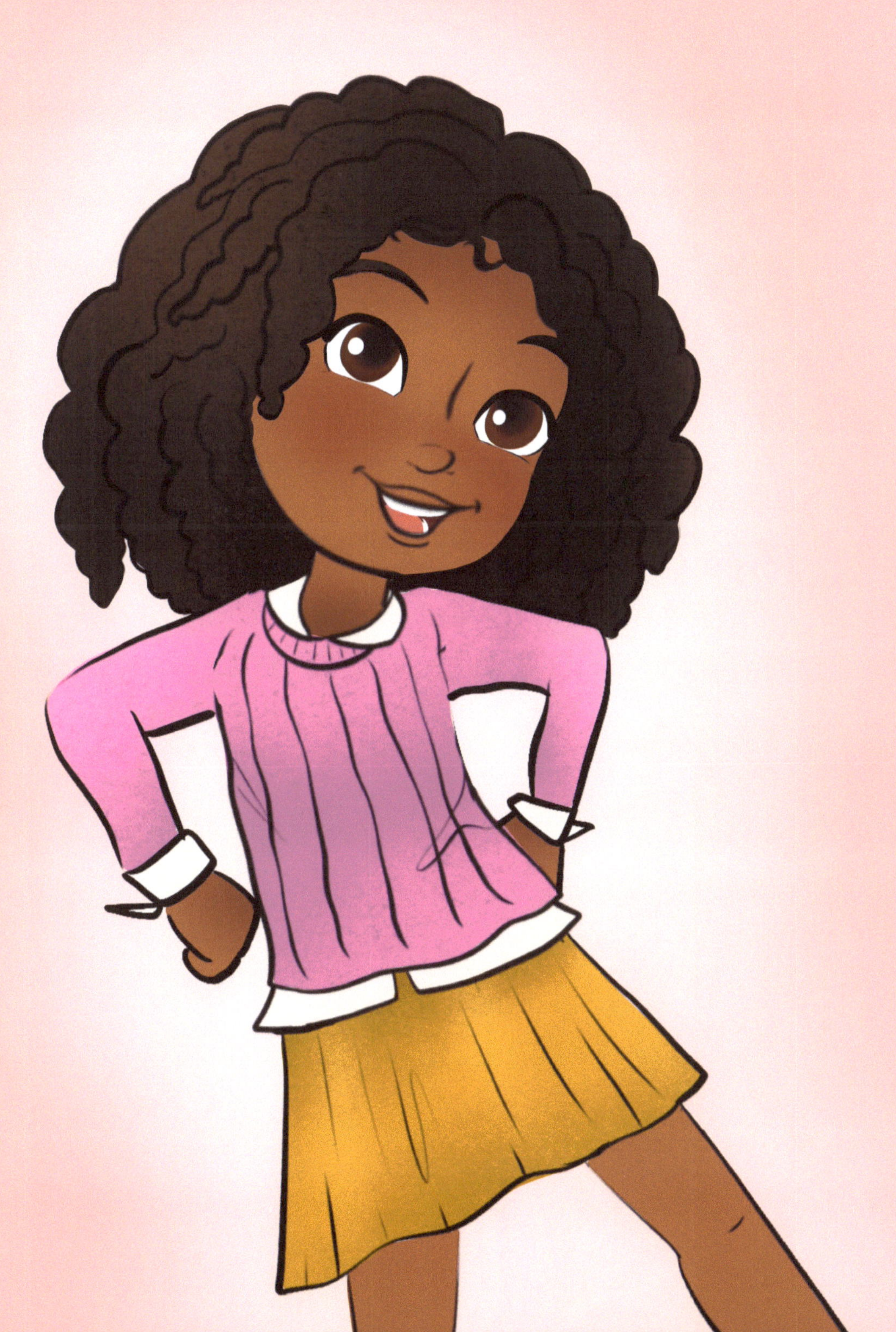

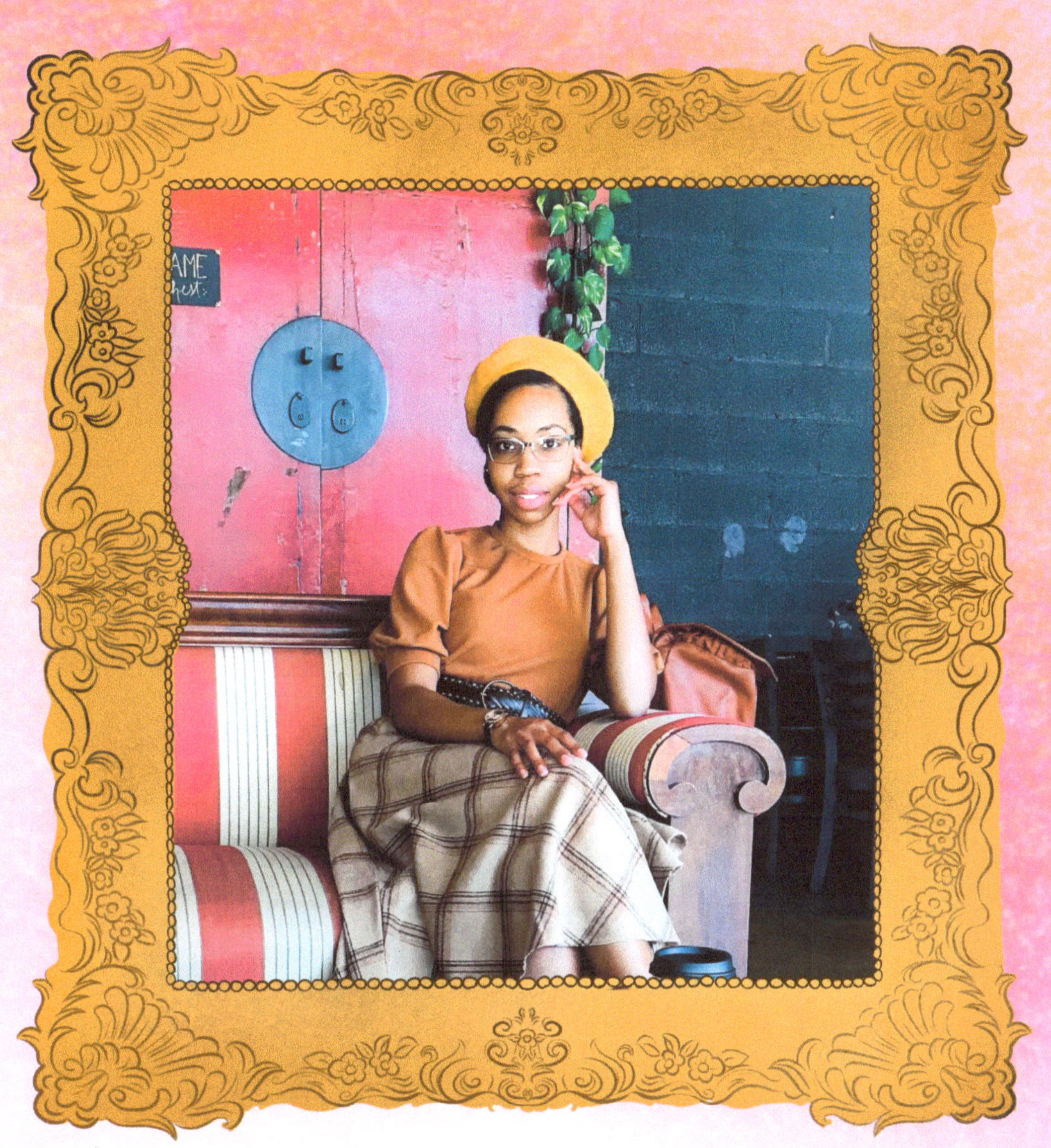

Tellie Simpson is the founder of
A Girl In A Museum World
and author of this endearing tale.
This book strives to motivate kids to take charge of their history and to follow their dreams, no matter what.
Visit www.agirlinamuseumworld.com

www.ingramcontent.com/pod-product-compliance
Lightning Source LLC
LaVergne TN
LVHW070206110826
845147LV00002B/516

* 9 7 9 8 9 8 5 6 2 6 8 0 3 *